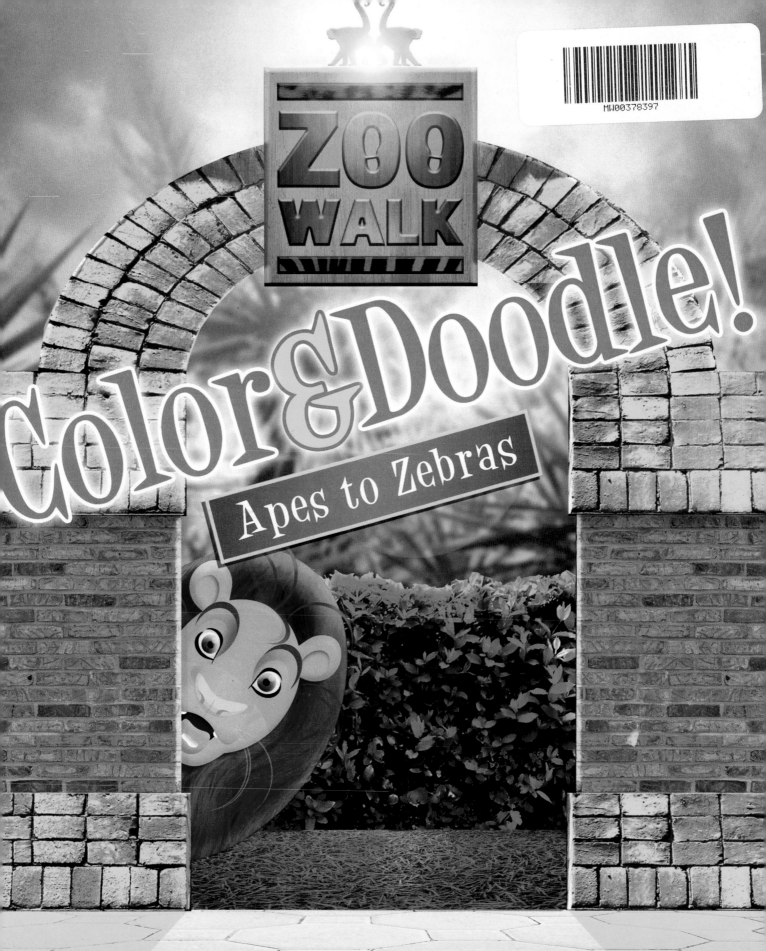

ZOO WALK

Color & Doodle!

Apes to Zebras

Created by
Daren Challman

Color & Doodle!

Apes to Zebras

Copyright © 2016

Daren Challman

All rights reserved.

ISBN 978-1-5327-5819-5

Dedicated to

Tina Hafzalla and her creative students

Welcome to your day here at the zoo!
The animals are excited and waiting for you!

A is for the ape
that likes to draw shapes.

Square   Circle   Triangle

Help the ape draw and color the shapes!

Star

Polygon

B is for the bear
that likes to point
and stare.

What is the bear pointing and staring at?

C is for the crocodile
bathing in the creek.
It smiles all the while
with its many, many teeth!

Give the crocodile a mouth full of teeth!

D is for the little deer
that has a silly thing to fear!

What is chasing the little deer?

E is for the elephant calf
that balances peanuts
to make the children laugh.

Draw the children laughing!

F is for the flamingo
that likes to play bingo.

Bingo is a game using numbers.
What number do you see
the pink flamingo's
legs making?

Is it 1, 2, 3, 4 or 5?

Trace and color the numbers! You can even creatively turn them into animals if you want to!

G is for the giraffe
with a neck sticking high.
Draw some singing birds
as they closely fly by.

H is for the hippopotamus
with an appetite so bottomless.

Color the fruits and vegetables!

I is for the insects, and wouldn't you know!
They enjoy playing games like Tic-Tac-Toe!

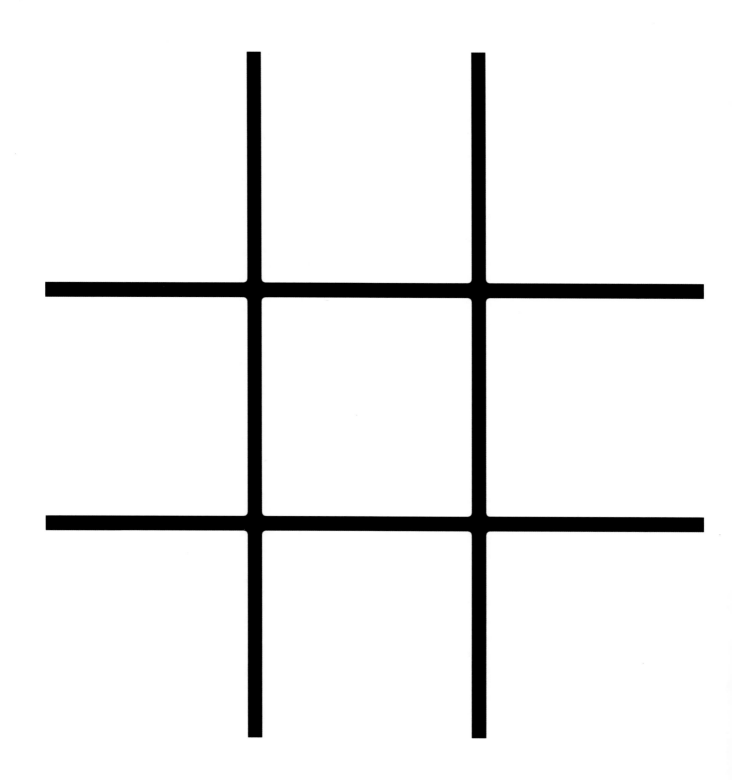

Carefully color and cut out the bugs and play!

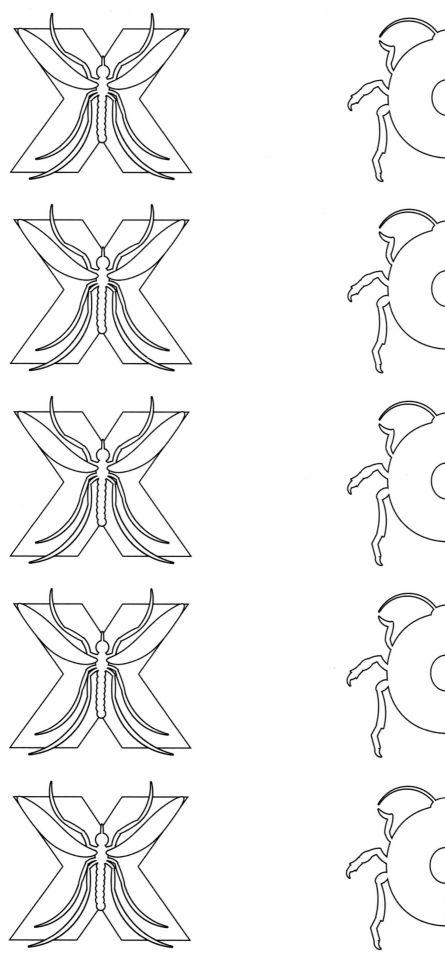

This page is intentionally left blank.

Draw *your* favorite zoo animal!

J is for the jaguar
with a coat of many spots.
Help reveal the object
by connecting the dots!

Connect the spots!

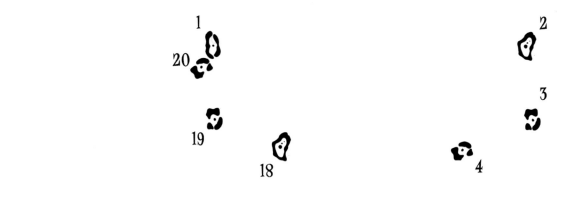

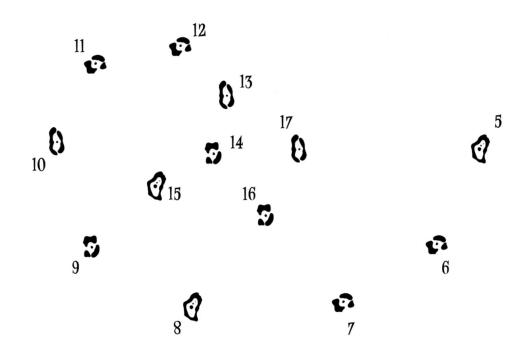

What do you see?

K is for the kangaroo
that bounces all around the zoo.

Help the kangaroo find its friend!

Start

End

L is for the lion
that roams a wide open space.
Help complete the picture
by finishing its face!

M is for the monkey
that swings from the vine . . .

Search for the words and see what you find!

```
C I E G W G D F I H G O A O Q
V R W F A H L O O R A G N A K
A C O G F A H L B C S E P A R
I G F C M A R X K I T P L Z I
T V Q I O F R W F F C M L Z X
P Q N L Y D Q I R E E Z C T P
Z G I Q T G I A G L S H C S N
O O H W F Z U L G E N E A S C
N Z T Z W G A Z E P I B D R G
Y F H M A W O A K H H G E G Q
W V Z J H I P P O A L V E A B
B H N P V B C P E N J L R S R
K D T G Y L Q R R T L F H A Z
Y E C X B K Y B X M H G R D M
R T C L M O L H L J B U I X E
```

APE   ELEPHANT   INSECTS
BEAR   FLAMINGO   JAGUAR
CROCODILE   GIRAFFE   KANGAROO
DEER   HIPPO   LION

N is for the newt
that sits rather cute,
but don't get too close
or it may have to scoot!

What is climbing toward the newt?

O is for the ostrich
hiding its head
in the sand . . .

Draw what it sees beneath where it stands.

P is for the penguin
that slides on the ice,
having friends all around
who play very nice.

What are some nice things you can do for a friend?

1. _____

   _____

2. _____

   _____

3. _____

   _____

4. _____

   _____

5. _____

   _____

6. _____

   _____

Q is for the quail
that likes to tell its tale.

Complete the quail's story
by filling in the blanks using
nouns, verbs, and adjectives.

I am a _____ quail. I spend all
(adjective)

my time at the _____. I enjoy it when
(noun)

the _____ come to visit. They make me
(plural noun)

very_____. There are times when I like
(adjective)

to _____ and _____ for
(verb)   (verb)

everyone. It makes them _____.
(adjective)

I hope to _____ you at the zoo!
(verb)

R is for the rhino
that comes upon a rainbow.

Draw the end of a rainbow touching the ground.
What are the colors of the rainbow?

S is for the spider
that carefully spins each strand,
It almost looks too easy
to spin a web so grand.

Help the spider create its fancy web!

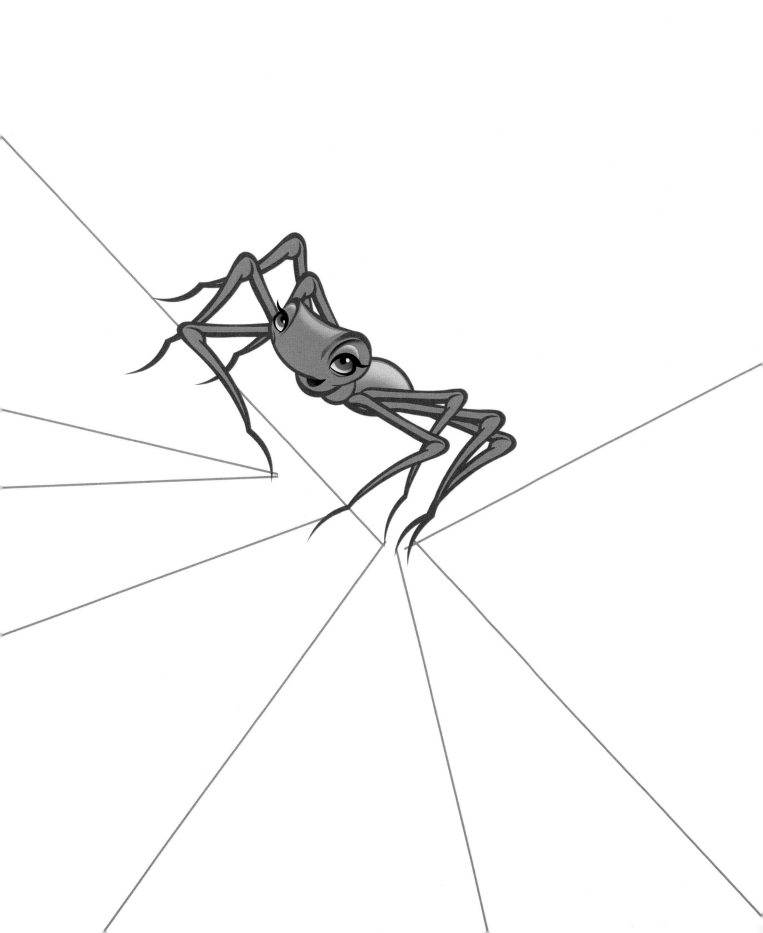

T is for the tiger
that never whines or gripes.
For anyone would be pleased
with such amazing stripes.

Draw the tiger's stripes!

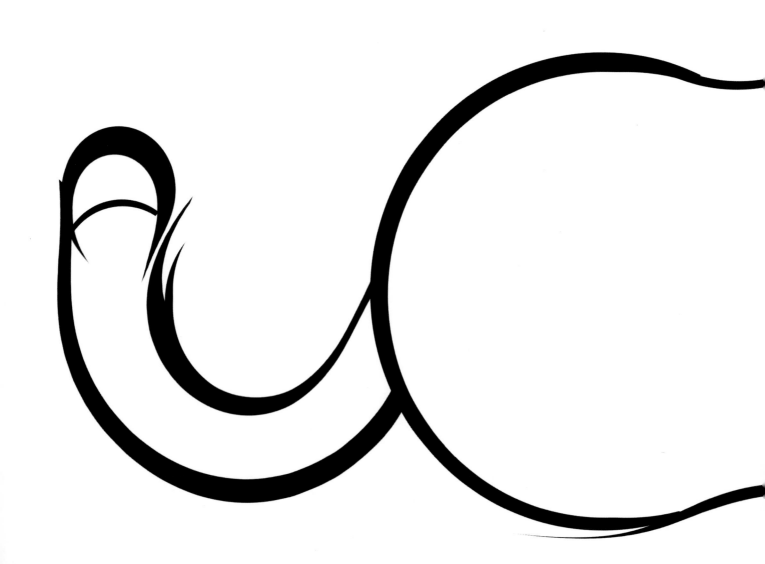

U is for the unicorn
which no one seems to see . . .

But you can draw the unicorn
as how you think it should be!

V is for the vulture
that dreams of its next meal.
For it's all it ever thinks about
as food is a big deal.

What kind of foods does the vulture dream about?
Draw them!

W is for the walrus
who smiles from dawn till dusk.
Its smile is quite noticable
with those two, large tusks.

What the walrus is smiling at? Draw it!

X marks the spot
where the animals gather a lot.

What other animals have come to join?
Draw and color them!

Y is for the generous yak
that carries friends upon its back.

What kind of animal friends are riding on the yak's back?
Are there any waiting in line? Draw them!

Z is for the zebra
letting us know
that it's almost time
for us to go.

What is one last animal or thing you would like to see at the zoo? Draw it!

The day at the zoo
has come to an end,
but the animals are sure
they will see you again!

Made in the USA
San Bernardino, CA
20 April 2020